SCOTT FORESMAN

ON YOUR MARK

WORKBOOK

1

INTRODUCTORY

Second Edition

Karen Davy

Workbook by Cheryl Pavlik

On Your Mark 1 Workbook, Second Edition

Pearson Education, 10 Bank Street, White Plains, NY 10606

Vice president, director of publishing: Allen Ascher
Editorial director: Louise Jennewine
Acquisitions editor: Bill Preston
Vice president, director of design and production: Rhea Banker
Development editor: Barbara Barysh
Production manager: Alana Zdinak
Production supervisor: Liza Pleva
Executive managing editor: Linda Moser
Production editor: Lynn Contrucci
Director of manufacturing: Patrice Fraccio
Senior manufacturing buyer: Edith Pullman
Photo research: Quarasan
Cover design: Charles Yuen
Text design and composition: Quarasan
Photo credits: p. 10, PhotoDisc, Inc. (1, 2, 5 across, 5 down, 7), Artville (3), Corel
    Corporation (4), Image provided by MetaTools (6); p. 15, PhotoDisc, Inc.; p. 20,
    PhotoDisc, Inc.; p. 22, Comstock, Inc.; p. 44, Neal Preston/CORBIS (top),
    Michael Newman/PhotoEdit (center), Jack Star/PhotoLink/PhotoDisc, Inc.
    (bottom); p. 46, PhotoDisc, Inc.; p. 47, PhotoDisc, Inc.; p. 57, PhotoDisc, Inc.
    (pizza, soup), Comstock, Inc. (hamburger, salad, hot dog, french fries),
    Paramount/Picture Quest (milk), Jess Alford/PhotoDisc, Inc. (chicken); p. 58,
    Artville; p. 59, PhotoDisc, Inc. (soup, pizza), Comstock, Inc. (french fries),
    Paramount/Picture Quest (milk), Jess Alford/PhotoDisc, Inc. (chicken); p. 69,
    Image Farm (1a, 2a, 3a, 3b, 4a, 6b); PhotoDisc, Inc. (2b, 5a, 5b, 6a); p. 82,
    PhotoDisc, Inc. (kicking, running), EyeWire (playing football, hitting ball,
    playing softball), Swoop/FPG (catching ball), Catherine Karnow/Woodfin
    Camp/Picture Quest (throwing Frisbee)
Illustrations: Scott Annis pp. 26 (top 1–6), 29; Ruta Daugavietis pp. 21, 64, 65, 66,
    70, 79; John Edwards p. 30; John Faulkner pp. 9, 16 (6 top, 4 bottom), 33, 34,
    38, 51, 52, 53, 76, 81, 85, 88; Tom R. Garcia pp. 4, 6, 7, 25, 32, 73, 77, 78, 84, 89,
    90, 91 (Practice 3), 94; Lane Gregory p. 26 (bottom 1–6); Al Hering pp. 27, 81
    (1, 2, 4, 7); Jared Lee pp. 17, 18, 23, 24, 41, 42, 49, 50, 54, 55; Scot Ritchie p. 91
    (Practice 4); Philip Scheuer p. 62; Gary Torrisi pp. 1, 8 (bottom 1–4), 14, 68, 75;
    Jeff Weyer pp. 72, 93
Cover photos: Jim Barber/The Stock Rep (keyboard), © 1999 David Lissy, All
    Rights Reserved (runner's foot), © Jim Westphalen (type)

ISBN 0-201-64578-5

1 2 3 4 5 6 7 8 9 10—BAH—05 04 03 02 01 00

Things to Do

Look at the pictures. Write the sentences.

> Close your book.   Look at the picture.
> Open your book.   Raise your hand.
> Repeat.   Sit down.
> *Stand up.*   Work with a partner.
> Write on the board.

1. _Stand up._

2. _____

3. _____

4. _____

5. _____

6. _____

7. _____

8. _____

9. _____

PRACTICE 1

Introduce yourself. Ask questions. Write a letter.

_____d_____ **1.** Hello. I'm Ted.   **a.** It's nice to meet you, too.

_____ **2.** What's your name?   **b.** Mexico

_____ **3.** It's nice to meet you.   **c.** Mrs. Cooke

_____ **4.** Where are you from?   **d.** Hi, I'm Yoshi.

PRACTICE 2

Look at the pictures. Circle the words.

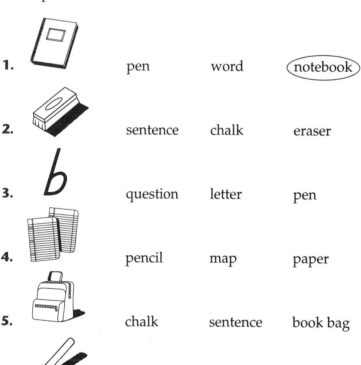

1.   pen   word   (notebook)

2.   sentence   chalk   eraser

3.   question   letter   pen

4.   pencil   map   paper

5.   chalk   sentence   book bag

6.   word   chalk   eraser

7.   pencil   pen   letter

PRACTICE 3

Listen. Circle the numbers.

a.	②	8	6
b.	1	3	9
c.	7	4	5
d.	1	8	4
e.	5	2	10
f.	7	2	1
g.	7	8	2
h.	3	9	4
i.	8	3	6
j.	9	5	4

PRACTICE 4

Write the number words.

1. 1 _____one_____
2. 0 _____
3. 5 _____
4. 8 _____
5. 7 _____
6. 2 _____
7. 4 _____
8. 3 _____
9. 10 _____
10. 6 _____
11. 9 _____

PRACTICE 5

Write the number words.

1. Six plus one is _____seven_____ .
2. Eight plus one is _____ .
3. Four plus _____ is ten.
4. _____ plus three is five.
5. One plus _____ is six.
6. _____ plus five is eight.

PRACTICE 6

🎧 Listen. Circle the letters.

1. p (f) q
2. h r e
3. g j y
4. n w m
5. v s w
6. h k c
7. e u a
8. w y l
9. y a e
10. x z k
11. o q p

PRACTICE 7

🎧 Listen. Write the letters.

1. _a_   7. _____
2. _____   8. _____
3. _____   9. _____
4. _____   10. _____
5. _____   11. _____
6. _____

PRACTICE 8

🎧 Listen. Write the words.

1. _your_   7. _____
2. _____   8. _____
3. _____   9. _____
4. _____   10. _____
5. _____   11. _____
6. _____

PRACTICE 9

A. Look at the pictures. Write the names.

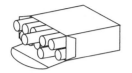

1. _____chalk_____   2. _____   3. _____

4. _____   5. _____

B. Circle the words in Part A.

a	q	b	o	o	k	o	e	i	g	h	t
o	k	r	y	s	x	n	g	p	m	f	w
c	h	a	l	k	o	e	u	f	o	u	r
n	o	z	k	o	r	e	a	c	i	e	t
u	n	i	t	e	d	s	t	a	t	e	s
b	d	l	t	g	m	m	e	x	i	c	o
j	e	o	w	y	a	u	m	k	v	p	e
p	s	g	o	p	c	h	a	i	r	e	s
v	k	l	e	t	c	o	l	d	i	n	i
x	z	e	r	o	i	l	a	x	r	s	x

C. Circle the names of six countries. Write the names.

1. _____Guatemala_____   4. _____

2. _____   5. _____

3. _____   6. _____

D. Circle six number words. Write the words.

1. _____eight_____   4. _____

2. _____   5. _____

3. _____   6. _____

Write the words.

1. A: Hi. I'm Maria. _____ your name?
It's/What's

B: _____ Yuri.
It's/What's

2. A: _____ this?
It's/What's

B: It's _____ eraser.
a/an

3. A: _____ this?
It's/What's

B: _____ chalk.
It's/What's

4. A: What's _____?
it's/this

B: It's _____ notebook.
a/an

 Listen. Circle the words.

1.	word	(window)	name
2.	name	number	notebook
3.	eraser	country	desk
4.	page	book	door
5.	pencil	letter	name
6.	book	pen	window
7.	eraser	board	door
8.	paper	pencil	book bag
9.	name	chalk	book
10.	notebook	name	word
11.	letter	paper	country

PRACTICE 12

Look at Ken. What's his first name? What's his last name?

My first name is Ken. My last name is Ono.

Name	
Ken	*Ono*
First	Last
Japan	
Country	

Look at Rosa. Write her first name. Write her last name.

My first name is Rosa. My last name is Sánchez.

Name	
First	Last
Mexico	
Country	

PRACTICE 13

Write your name and country.

Name	
First	Last
Country	

PRACTICE 14

Write the answers. Use sentences.

1. What's your first name? _____
2. What's your last name? _____
3. Where are you from? _____

 **Check Your Knowledge**

Vocabulary Check

A. Look at the pictures. Write the words.

1. _____chalk_____

2. _____

3. _____

4. _____

5. _____

6. _____

B. Write the numbers.

1. two	_2_	**5.** three	_____	**9.** six	_____
2. seven	_____	**6.** eight	_____	**10.** one	_____
3. four	_____	**7.** five	_____	**11.** zero	_____
4. ten	_____	**8.** nine	_____		

Check Your Understanding

Look at the pictures. Write *What's* or *It's*.

1. A: _____*What's*_____ this?

B: _____ a paper.

2. A: _____ this?

B: _____ an eraser.

3. A: _____ your name?

B: Carol Brown.

4. A: _____ this?

B: _____ a notebook.

PRACTICE 1

Look at the pictures. Circle the words.

1.   number   eraser   (notebook)

2.   window   table   chair

3.   woman   boy   man

4.   book bag   book   wastebasket

5.   boy   woman   man

6.   locker   door   desk

7.   notebook   table   wastebasket

8.   girl   boy   man

9.   chalk   chair   locker

Look at the pictures. Write the words.

	1 m	2 e		n			3		

Across →

1.

4.

5.

7.

Down ↓

2.

3.

5.

6.

Listen. Circle the numbers.

a. ⑪   8   13
b. 14   20   12
c. 19   15   13
d. 20   12   10
e. 16   8   18
f. 17   16   19
g. 13   14   17
h. 10   11   14
i. 17   15   7
j. 19   10   16

PRACTICE 4

Write the number words.

1. 14 ___*fourteen*___
2. 18 _____
3. 20 _____
4. 13 _____
5. 17 _____
6. 11 _____
7. 10 _____
8. 19 _____
9. 15 _____
10. 12 _____
11. 16 _____

PRACTICE 5

Write the number words.

1. Fifteen minus two is ___*thirteen*___.
2. Sixteen minus five is _____.
3. _____ minus four is sixteen.
4. Twenty minus _____ is three.
5. _____ minus fourteen is four.
6. _____ minus two is seventeen.

PRACTICE 6

Listen. Write the words.

1. _____table_____   5. _____   9. _____

2. _____   6. _____   10. _____

3. _____   7. _____   11. _____

4. _____   8. _____

PRACTICE 7

Write the singular or plural noun.

Singular	Plural	Singular	Plural
1. pen	pens	5. girl	
2.	women	6. man	
3.	lockers	7.	books
4. chair		8.	boys

PRACTICE 8

What's this? What are these?

Write *It's* or *They're*.

1. _____It's_____ a wastebasket.

2. _____ a locker.

3. _____ chairs.

4. _____ a table.

5. _____ books.

| What's | this | It's |
| What are | these | They're |

Write the correct words.

1. A: _____*What are*_____ these?

   B: _____ pens.

2. A: _____ this?

   B: _____ a pen.

3. A: What's _____?

   B: _____ a wastebasket.

4. A: _____ these?

   B: _____ erasers.

5. A: What are _____?

   B: _____ notebooks.

Where's the notebook?

Write *in*, *on*, or *under*.

1. It's _____*in*_____ the wastebasket.

2. It's _____ the chair.

3. It's _____ the book bag.

4. It's _____ the table.

PRACTICE 11

Listen. Circle the sentences.

1. (It's on the desk.)   It's under the desk.
2. It's in the desk.   It's on the desk.
3. It's under the wastebasket. It's in the wastebasket.
4. It's on the locker.   It's in the locker.
5. It's on the chair.   It's under the chair.
6. It's on the book bag.   It's in the book bag.

PRACTICE 12

Answer the questions. Write *in, on,* or *under*.

1. Where's the book?   _It's in the book bag._
2. Where's the notebook?   _____
3. Where's the pen?   _____
4. Where is the book bag?   _____
5. Where's the man?   _____
6. Where are the pencils?   _____

Unit 2

14

PRACTICE 13

Fill in the Student ID Card. Use Amy's information.

Her name is Amy Chin.

Her address is 869 Mar Vista Avenue, Dallas, Texas 75211.

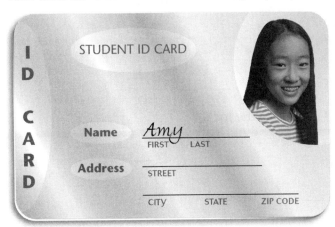

PRACTICE 14

Look at Abdul's Student ID Card. Answer the questions. Use sentences.

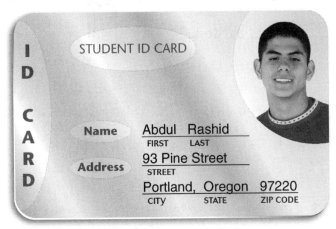

1. What's his first name?

_____

2. What's his last name?

_____

3. What's his address?

_____

_____

Check Your Knowledge

Vocabulary Check

Look at the pictures. Write the correct words.

book bag	papers	in
book	pencils	on
chair	wastebasket	under

1. The _____*chair*_____ is _____*on*_____ the locker.

2. The _____ is _____ the desk.

3. The _____ is _____ the table.

4. The _____ are _____ the desk.

5. The _____ is _____ the chair.

6. The _____ are _____ the wastebasket.

Check Your Understanding

Look at the pictures. Circle the correct questions.

1. What's this?
   (What are these?)

2. What's this?
   What are these?

3. What's this?
   What are these?

4. What's this?
   What are these?

PRACTICE 1

Look at the pictures. Circle the words.

1.   library   (cafeteria)   office

2.   class   restroom   gym

3.   library   gym   cafeteria

4.   office   restroom   class

5.   gym   library   office

6.   restroom   office   class

Look at the pictures. Write the names.

Mrs. Park

Ms. Davis

Mr. García

Mr. Habib

Marta

Mrs. White

1. _____Mr. García_____ is the principal.
2. _____ is the PE teacher.
3. _____ is the librarian.
4. _____ is a student.
5. _____ is the cashier.
6. _____ is the English teacher.

PRACTICE 3

Listen. Circle the numbers.

a.	20	30	(60)	**f.**	93	23	73
b.	42	52	82	**g.**	47	77	52
c.	86	36	46	**h.**	67	37	27
d.	31	91	81	**i.**	89	29	39
e.	51	56	66	**j.**	64	74	54

PRACTICE 4

Write the number words.

1. 20 _____twenty_____

2. 70 _____

3. 90 _____

4. 80 _____

5. 62 _____

6. 44 _____

7. 38 _____

8. 56 _____

9. 22 _____

10. 81 _____

11. 93 _____

PRACTICE 5

Write the number words.

1. Twenty times two is _____forty_____.

2. Five times five is _____.

3. Six times seven is _____.

4. Nine times _____ is ninety.

5. Eight times nine is _____.

6. Three times _____ is sixty.

7. _____ times two is fifty-six.

A. Write the names of the people and places.

1. f o f i e c   <u>o</u> <u>f</u> <u>f</u> <u>i</u> (<u>c</u>) <u>e</u>

2. y l a r r b i   — — — — Ⓞ — —

3. a h c s e i r   — — — Ⓞ — — —

4. e f i c r a t e a   — — — Ⓞ — Ⓞ — —

5. d e s u n t t   — — — — Ⓞ Ⓞ

B. Write the letters in the circles.

— — — — — — —

C. Look at the picture. Answer the question. Use the letters in Part B.

Who's Mr. Sánchez?

He's a _____.

PRACTICE 7

Write the contractions. Write the words.

		Contraction			Contraction
1.	he is	*he's*	**5.**		she's
2.	who is		**6.**	they are	
3.		I'm	**7.**	it is	
4.	you are		**8.**		what's

Complete the sentences. Use the verb *be* with *I, he, she,* and *they*. Use contractions.

1. **A:** Where ___is___ David?

B: ___He's___ in the library.

2. **A:** Where _____ Mario and Kim?

B: _____ in the gym.

3. **A:** Who _____ you?

B: _____ an English teacher.

4. **A:** Who _____ Ms. Halsted?

B: _____ the principal.

5. **A:** Who's _____?

B: _____ Mrs. Garcia. _____ the PE teacher.

6. **A:** Who _____ _____?

B: _____ Mr. Lee and Mrs. Jones. _____ librarians.

Listen. Write the address or phone number.

1. Library: ___182-6656___

2. Mrs. Chen: _____

3. Gold's Gym: _____ River Road

4. Gloria: _____

5. Kim's address: _____ Oak Road

6. Mr. García: _____

7. Mr. García's address: _____ Fair Street

8. Ted: _____

Read the names, addresses, and phone numbers. Answer the questions.

Chen Tina	1900 Lake Street	 555-9826
Halsted Diane	634 Clark Street	 136-7491
Johnson Gloria	1245 School Street	 555-3818
Lu Peter	546 Wood Street	 184-3890
Mendoza Jorge	690 Beach Drive	 274-7274
Sánchez Mario	6237 Buena Vista	 555-2648

1. What's Peter's address?

    546 Wood Street

2. What's Ms. Halsted's phone number?

3. What's Gloria's phone number?

4. What's Tina's address?

5. What's Mario's phone number?

6. What's Mr. Mendoza's address?

7. What's Gloria's address?

Read Mario's ID card. Write about his name, address, and phone number.

Name __Mario__ __Sánchez__
      First   Last

Address __6237 Buena Vista__

__Miami, Florida__ __33156__
  City   State   ZIP Code

Phone Number __(305)555-2648__
              Area Code

His name is _____

_____

_____

_____

Check Your Knowledge

Vocabulary Check

Who are the people? Where are they?

Look at the pictures. Complete the sentences. Use the verb *be* and *he, she,* and *they.* Use contractions.

1. **A:** Who _____*is*_____ she?
   B: _____*She's*_____ Mayka Lu. _____
   a _____.

Mayka Lu

2.

   Mr. Miller

   A: Who _____ he?
   B: _____ Mr. Miller. _____
   a PE _____.

3. **A:** Who _____ they?
   B: _____ Mr. Chang and Mrs. Wilson.
   _____ are _____.

   Mr. Chang
   and Mrs. Wilson

4. **A:** Where _____ Raul?
   B: _____ in the _____.

   Raul

5. **A:** Where _____ Tina and Ricardo?
   B: _____ in the _____.

   Tina and Ricardo

Check Your Understanding

Read about Mayka. Fill out the student ID card for her.

My name is Mayka Lu. My student number is 936-87-3781. My phone number is (608) 111-4392. My address is 245 Maple Avenue, Madison, Wisconsin 53704.

PARKER SCHOOL

STUDENT ID CARD

I D   C A R D

Student Number _____

NAME _____
FIRST   LAST

ADDRESS _____
STREET

_____
CITY   STATE   ZIP CODE

PHONE ( ) _____
AREA CODE

Unit 3

24

PRACTICE 1

Look at the pictures. Circle the words.

1. (family)   mother   daughter

2. son   father   mother

3. daughter   son   father

4. mother   son   daughter

5. daughter   father   mother

6. sisters   mothers   brothers

7. brothers   fathers   sisters

8. grandmother   grandfather   son

9. grandfather   mother   father

PRACTICE 2

Write the names of the places.

1. _bedroom_

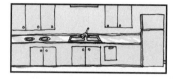

2. _____

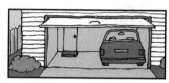

3. _____

4. _____

5. _____

6. _____

PRACTICE 3

Complete the sentences.

brother	husband	sister	wife
daughter	mother	son	

1. I'm Gloria's daughter.

Gloria is my ___mother___.

2. I'm Bob's sister.

Bob is my _____.

3. I'm Jim's wife.

Jim is my _____.

4. I'm David's mother.

David is my _____.

5. I'm Claudia's husband.

Claudia is my _____.

6. I'm Angela's father.

Angela is my _____.

PRACTICE 4

Complete the conversation with the correct possessive adjectives.

PATRICIA: This is my family, Roberto. Look at the pictures.
She's **(1.)** __my__ mother. **(2.)** _____
name is Isabel. He's my father. **(3.)** _____
name is Jim. They're my grandparents.
(4.) _____ names are Dino and Leah.
And that's my cat.

ROBERTO: What's **(5.)** _____ name?

PATRICIA: Buster.

ROBERTO: Buster? Oh. And who are they, Patricia?

PATRICIA: They're **(6.)** _____ sister and brother. They're in the yard.

ROBERTO: And what's this?

PATRICIA: That's **(7.)** _____ home.

ROBERTO: **(8.)** _____ pictures are great!

PATRICIA: Thanks!

PRACTICE 5

Write the correct words.

1. ___I'm___ Roberto. Linda is _____ mother. _____ fifty.
      I'm/My   I'm/my   She's/Her

2. My grandmother's name is Maria. _____ daughter is _____ mother.
                                           She/Her   I/my

3. My brother is twenty-six. _____ name is Miguel. _____ a librarian.
                            He's/His   He's/His

4. _____ seventeen. _____ a student at Harrison School.
      I'm/My   I'm/My

5. Tom and Matt are students, too. _____ brothers. _____ last name is Custer.
                        They're/Their   They're / Their

6. _____ in English class. _____ teacher is Mr. Chen.
    We're/Our   We're/Our

7. Who's in _____ class? What are _____ names?
        you're/your   they're/their

PRACTICE 6

Complete the questions. Write the correct words.

1. A: _____*Is she*_____ in your class?

B: Yes, she is.

2. A: _____ Mr. Tanaka?

B: No, he isn't. He's Mr. Kato.

3. A: _____ in his class?

B: Yes, I am.

4. A: _____ your parents?

B: Yes, they are.

5. A: _____ and your parents from Mexico?

B: No, we're not. We're from Guatemala.

6. A: _____ in the yard?

B: No, it isn't. It's in the garage.

PRACTICE 7

Complete the answers. Write the correct word or words.

1. A: Is your last name Walter?

B: No, it _____*isn't*_____. _____*It's*_____ Walker.

2. A: Are you a student?

B: Yes, _____.

3. A: Is he your teacher?

B: No, he _____. _____ the principal.

4. A: Are they your parents?

B: Yes, they _____.

5. A: Are you Raymond's sister?

B: No, _____. _____ his mother.

6. A: Are your brothers teachers?

B: No, they _____. _____ students.

7. A: Are you and Ken brothers?

B: Yes, we _____.

8. A: Is it your cat?

B: Yes, it _____.

Read the words. Write the contractions.

1. she is _____*she's*_____   **5.** it is _____

2. I am _____   **6.** he is _____

3. are not _____   **7.** they are _____

4. we are _____   **8.** is not _____

PRACTICE **9**

Look at the pictures. Write questions and answers.

1. Emilia/bedroom

Is Emilia in the bedroom _____?

No, she isn't. She's in the living room.

2. Paul/kitchen

_____?

_____

3. Henry/garage

_____?

_____

4. Julie and Greg/kitchen

_____?

_____

5. the girls/yard

_____?

_____

6. the cat/bedroom

_____?

_____

7. you/library

_____?

_____

Read the names of the people in Juan's family.

| Ana | Tina | Lucy |
| Victor | Paco | Tim |

Listen and write the names under the pictures.

Juan

 **PRACTICE 11**

Read about Karen and her family. Complete their information card.

   My name is Karen Carter. I am 16 years old. My father's name is Carl. He is 41 years old. My mother's name is Judith. She is 44. My brother's name is Craig, and my sister's name is Beth. Craig is 15, and Beth is 8. Our address is 991 Water Street, Chicago, Illinois 60656. Our phone number is (312) 555-4071.

Woodside School District Information Card

The ___Carter___ Family

Father's Name: _____ Age: _____

Mother's Name: _____ Age: _____

Children

    Name: _____ Age: _____

    Name: _____ Age: _____

    Name: _____ Age: _____

Address: _____

_____

Phone: _____

PRACTICE 12

Read Paul's information card. Write about Paul and his family.

Metro High School Family Information Card

The ___Jordan___ Family

Father's Name: ___Dennis___ Age: _48_

Mother's Name: ___Elena___ Age: _42_

Children

    Name: ___Susan___ Age: _20_

    Name: ___Paul___ Age: _17_

    Name: ___David___ Age: _13_

Address: ___451 Taylor Ave.___

___Omaha, Nebraska 68105___

Phone: ___(402) 981-4266___

His name is _____

_____

_____

_____

_____

Check Your Knowledge

Vocabulary Check

Look at the Martinez family.
Complete the sentences.

brother	daughter	father	wife	sister
grandparents	husband	mother	parents	son

1. Sandra is Pablo's _____*sister*_____.

2. Alex is Ella's _____.

3. Leo is Ella's _____.

4. Alex and Anita are Pablo's _____.

5. Sandra is Anita's _____.

6. Anita is Alex's _____.

Leo   **Ella**

Alex   **Anita**

Pablo   **Sandra**

THE MARTINEZ FAMILY

Check Your Understanding

A. Complete the sentences about Sandra and her family.

1. I'm   my

_____*My*_____ name is Sandra. _____ 15 years old.

_____ a student.

2. he's   his

_____ my brother. _____ 18 years old.

_____ name is Pablo.

3. we're   our

_____ father is Alex. _____ mother is Anita.

_____ their children.

4. they're   their

_____ our grandparents. _____ first names are Leo

and Ella. _____ last name is Martinez.

B. Look at the Martinez family in Vocabulary Check. Write Sandra's answers
to the questions about her and her family.

1. Is Leo your father? *No, he isn't. He's my grandfather.* _____

2. Is Anita your mother? _____

3. Are Leo and Ella your grandparents? _____

4. Are you 25 years old? _____

5. Is your name Sandra? _____

PRACTICE 1

Look at the pictures. Circle the words.

1. math (lunch) science

2. science math social studies

3. computer lunch math

4. science math lunch

5. math computer science

6. lunch computer PE

PRACTICE 2

A. Look at the pictures. Read the names. Complete the sentences.

Ted and Dan

Krista

Pedro

Kate

Jack

Kevin and Mike

1. _____Jack is_____ in computer class.
2. _____ in science class.
3. _____ in social studies class.
4. _____ at lunch in the cafeteria.
5. _____ in math class.
6. _____ in PE class.

B. Look at the pictures in Part A. Ask and answer questions. Use sentences.

1. Where is Jack?

   _____

2. _____

   They're in PE class.

3. Where are Ted and Dan?

   _____

4. Where is Krista?

   _____

Listen. Circle the correct clocks.

1. a. 6:15   b. 6:51

2. a.   b.

3. a. 4:30   b.

4. a. 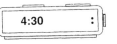   b. 5:45

5. a. 2:40   b.

6. a. 9:45   b.

7. a.   b. 12:35

8. a. 8:10   b.

9. a. 2:22   b.

10. a.   b. 6:05

Unit 5

35

PRACTICE 4

Look at the clocks. Draw the time. Write the numbers.

1. It's ten after four.

2. It's one thirty.

3. It's three fifteen.

4. It's a quarter to eight.

5. It's nine fifteen.

6. It's three fifty-five.

PRACTICE 5

What time is it?

Look at the clocks. Write two sentences with the same meaning.

a. _It's two ten._
       It's ten after two.

b. _____

7:45

       _____

c. _____
       _____

1:23

d. _____
       _____

PRACTICE 6

Complete the sentences. Write the correct words.

A. **do**   **does**

JUAN: What time **(1.)** _____do_____ you **(2.)** _____ your

homework?

MIKO: I **(3.)** _____ my homework at 7:00. What about you?

JUAN: I **(4.)** _____ my homework after school. When

(5.) _____ your brother **(6.)** _____ his

homework?

MIKO: At 9:00. He **(7.)** _____ it in his bedroom. Where

(8.) _____ your sisters **(9.)** _____ their

homework?

JUAN: They **(10.)** _____ it in their bedrooms, too.

B. **do**   **does**   **go**   **goes**

JUNKO: Where **(1.)** _____does_____ your brother **(2.)** _____go_____ to

school?

PAUL: He **(3.)** _____ to Harrison School. Where

(4.) _____ your sisters **(5.)** _____ to school?

JUNKO: They **(6.)** _____ to Metro High School. What time

(7.) _____ your brother **(8.)** _____ to school?

PAUL: He **(9.)** _____ to school at 8:00.

JUNKO: I **(10.)**_____ to school at 8:00, too. What about you? When

(11.) _____ you **(12.)** _____ to school?

PAUL: I **(13.)** _____ to school at 7:45.

C. **do**   **does**   **have**   **has**

RUDY: When **(1.)** _____do_____ you **(2.)** _____have_____ lunch, Sally?

SALLY: At 11:45, Rudy.

RUDY: Oh. When **(3.)** _____ Ted and Kate **(4.)** _____

lunch?

SALLY: Let's see . . . They **(5.)** _____ lunch at 11:45.

RUDY: And Dana? When **(6.)** _____ she **(7.)** _____

lunch?

SALLY: Oh, Dana **(8.)** _____ lunch at 11:45, too. What about you?

RUDY: Me? I **(9.)** _____ lunch then, too.

SALLY: Great!

PRACTICE 7

A. This is Gino's schedule. Listen. Write the class times.

	Time	Class	Room
Lincoln High School Class Schedule			
Name: Gino Alda			
1.	_8:15_	Science	102
2.	_____	PE	Gym
3.	_____	English	213
4.	_____	Lunch	Cafeteria
5.	_____	Math	310
6.	_____	Social Studies	201

B. Read Gino's schedule. Answer the questions. Write sentences.

1. Where does Gino have science class?

    He has science class in room 102.

2. What time does he have PE?

_____

3. When does he have English?

_____

4. Where does he have lunch?

_____

5. What time does he have math class?

_____

6. Where does he go to school?

_____

A. Read about Gino's daily routine. Write the times.

My name is Gino Alda. I get up at 7:00. At 7:30, I have breakfast. I go to school at 8:00. I have lunch at 12. At 3:30, I go home. I have dinner at 6:30. I do my homework at 7:30 or 8:00. At 10:30, I go to bed.

Name: *Gino Alda*

7:00 get up		_____ go home
_____ breakfast		_____ dinner
_____ go to school		_____ homework
_____ lunch		_____ go to bed

B. Read Junko's daily routine. Write about her routine.

Name: Junko Yamamoto

6:45 get up		3:15 go home
7:15 breakfast		6:00 dinner
8:00 go to school		7:00 homework
12:00 lunch		10:00 go to bed

Her name is Junko Yamamoto. She gets up at _____

_____

_____

_____

_____

Check Your Knowledge

Vocabulary Check

Read Pablo's schedule. Complete the sentences with the correct class or time.

Barton School Class Schedule			
Name: Pablo Reyes			
Time	**Class**	**Time**	**Class**
8:30	Math	12:00	Lunch
9:25	English	12:45	Science
10:20	Computer	1:55	Social Studies
11:10	PE		

Pablo goes to Barton School. This is his class schedule. He has six classes.

His first class is math. At **(1.)** _____ _8:30_ _____ he's in math class. He has

(2.) _____ class at 9:25. He has **(3.)** _____ class at 10:20.

At **(4.)** _____, he has lunch. At 12:45, he has **(5.)** _____.

He has **(6.)** _____ at 11:10. His last class is **(7.)** _____.

It's at **(8.)** _____.

Check Your Understanding

Read the answers. Complete the questions.

1. **A:** _____ _What time do_ _____ you _____ _have_ _____ lunch?
   B: I have lunch at 12:30.

2. **A:** _____ you _____ your homework?
   B: I do my homework after school.

3. **A:** _____ Pablo and Joe _____ their homework?
   B: They do their homework in the library.

4. **A:** _____ the students _____ home?
   B: They go home at 4:00 or 4:30.

5. **A:** _____ Lena _____ dinner?
   B: She has dinner at 7:00.

6. **A:** _____ Jack _____ to bed?
   B: He goes to bed at 11:00.

WHAT DO YOU DO ON THE WEEKEND?

PRACTICE **1**

Look at the pictures. Circle the words.

1. music   (art)   band

2. basketball   baseball   soccer

3. music   art   movies

4. basketball   band   baseball

5. basketball   baseball   soccer

6. park   art   movies

7. art   band   movies

8. shopping mall   library   park

PRACTICE 2

A. Answer the questions. Write the day of the week in the notebook.

	Monday		Wednesday			Saturday

1. What day comes after Monday? _____
2. What day comes after Saturday? _____
3. What day comes before Saturday? _____
4. What day comes after Wednesday? _____

B. Complete the box. Write the day of the week or the short form.

Day of the Week	Short Form	Day of the Week	Short form
Wednesday		Thursday	
	Sun.		Mon.
Tuesday		Saturday	
	Fri.		

PRACTICE 3

at baseball practice	at soccer practice
in art class	in music class
at the movies	

Look at the pictures. Write sentences. Use the activities from the box.

1. _She's at baseball practice_.

2. _____.

3. _____.

4. _____.

Unit 6

PRACTICE 4

Look at Jon's schedule. Complete the questions and answers.

Monday
  go to English class

Tuesday
  go to band practice

Wednesday
  go to the library

Thursday
  go to English class

Friday
  have soccer practice

Saturday
  have baseball practice

Sunday
  do homework

1. **A:** What _____does_____ Jon do on _____Wednesday_____?
   B: He _____ to the library.

2. **A:** What _____ Jon do on Friday?
   B: He has _____.

3. **A:** What _____ Jon do on _____?
   B: _____ baseball practice.

4. **A:** What _____ Jon do on Monday and Thursday?
   B: He _____.

5. **A:** What _____?
   B: He goes to band practice.

6. **A:** _____ on Sunday?
   B: On Sunday, _____.

Complete the sentences. Write the correct words.

1. **watch   watches**

   a. My brother _____*watches*_____ TV in the afternoon.

   b. You _____ TV at night.

   c. My sisters _____ TV at night, too.

2. **listen   listens**

   a. We _____ to music every weekend.

   b. Our teacher _____ to music in the evening.

   c. Clara _____ to music after school.

3. **read   reads**

   a. My mother _____ the newspaper every morning.

   b. Franco _____ the newspaper on Monday.

   c. I _____ the newspaper on Sunday.

4. **eat   eats**

   a. You _____ breakfast before school.

   b. They _____ breakfast at 10:00.

   c. Dan _____ breakfast every day.

5. **write   writes**

   a. We _____ letters on Saturday.

   b. Dan and Krista _____ letters after school.

   c. You _____ letters every weekend.

6. **study   studies**

   a. My sister _____ every day.

   b. I _____ in the library after school.

   c. My brother _____ on Sunday evening.

7. **work   works**

   a. Suki _____ at the mall after school.

   b. Eva _____ at the mall in the evening.

   c. They _____ at the mall on Saturday, too.

PRACTICE 6

Read the words. Write sentences.

I	watch/watches TV		the weekend
He	eat/eats lunch	at	the morning
Tina	do/does homework	in	the afternoon
You	play/plays soccer	on	Tuesday
We	have/has class		night
Amy and Pete	listen/listens to music		the evening

1. *I do homework in the afternoon.*

2. _____

3. _____

4. _____

5. _____

6. _____

7. _____

PRACTICE 7

Read the words. Write sentences.

1. read the newspaper / I / in the morning / never

    I never read the newspaper in the morning.

    In the morning, I never read the newspaper.

2. never / on Sunday / go to school / we

    _____

    _____

3. in the evening / work at the mall / always / they

    _____

    _____

4. always / Tim / studies in the library / on the weekend

    _____

    _____

5. has English class / at night / Kate / never

    _____

    _____

PRACTICE 8

Listen. Fill in Ted's schedule. Write an ✗.

	Sunday	Monday	Tuesday	Wednesday	Thursday	Friday	Saturday
Band							
Baseball	✗						
Basketball							
Homework							
Library							
Soccer							

PRACTICE 9

Read about Anna. Complete her schedule.

My name is Anna Wong. I am busy on the weekend. On Saturday morning, I go to art class. In the afternoon, I play basketball. I always go to the movies on Saturday night. On Sunday morning, I always read the newspaper. I do homework in the afternoon. At night, I listen to music.

Anna's Weekend Schedule

	Saturday	Sunday
Morning	go to art class	
Afternoon		
Night		

PRACTICE 10

Complete the schedule about your weekend. Write about yourself.

My Weekend Schedule

	Saturday	**Sunday**
Morning		
Afternoon		
Night		

My name is _____

_____

_____

_____

_____

_____

PRACTICE 11

Ask five students this question: *What do you do on Saturday?* Write sentences about their schedules.

Examples:

Mieko goes to the movies on Saturday.

On Saturday, Julie plays soccer.

1. _____

2. _____

3. _____

4. _____

5. _____

Check Your Knowledge

Vocabulary Check

Read Lin's schedule for Thursday, Friday, and Saturday. Complete the sentences with the correct word or words.

	Thursday	Friday	Saturday
Morning	have English class	have English class	play soccer
Afternoon	go to art class	go to band practice	go to the shopping mall
Evening	have basketball practice	study in library	go to movies with Mei
Night	do homework	watch TV with Mei	listen to music

Lin is always busy **(1.)** _____on_____ Thursday. She has English class **(2.)** _____ the morning. She goes to **(3.)** _____ in the afternoon. In the evening, she always **(4.)** _____ basketball practice. **(5.)** _____ night, she does homework.

Lin is busy **(6.)** _____ Friday, too. She has English class in the **(7.)** _____. In the afternoon, she always goes to **(8.)** _____. She **(9.)** _____ in the library in the evening. On Friday night, Lin and her sister Mei **(10.)** _____ TV.

Check Your Understanding

Write about Lin's schedule on Saturday.

___Lin is busy on Saturday, too. She___ _____

_____

_____

_____

_____

PRACTICE 1

Match the sentences with the pictures. Write the correct letter.

1. ___c___ He's happy.
2. _____ She's sick.
3. _____ He feels terrible.
4. _____ They're tired.
5. _____ They're thirsty.
6. _____ He's hungry.
7. _____ She's sad.

a.

b.

c.

d.

e.

f.

g.

Match the words with the part of the body. Write the correct letter.

1. ___h___ finger
2. _____ toe
3. _____ stomach
4. _____ back
5. _____ head
6. _____ arm
7. _____ foot
8. _____ hand
9. _____ leg
10. _____ throat

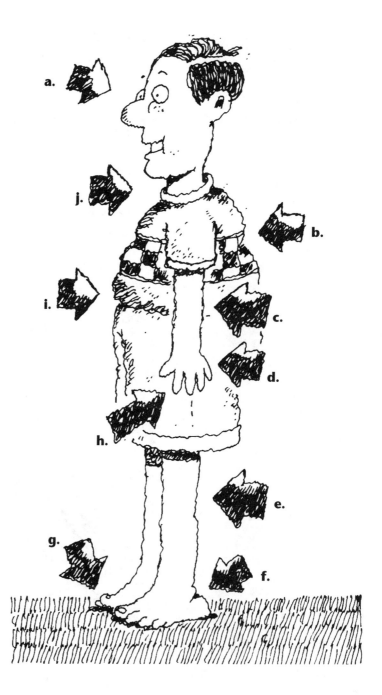

PRACTICE 3

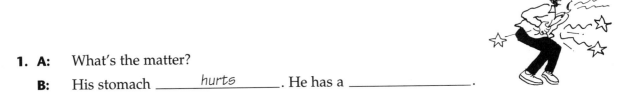

hurts   sore
backache   headache
stomachache

Complete the conversations. Use the words in the box.

1. **A:** What's the matter?

   B: His stomach _____*hurts*_____. He has a _____.

2. **A:** What's the matter?

   B: She has a _____ arm. Her arm _____.

3. **A:** How does she feel?

   B: Her back _____. She has a _____.

4. **A:** How does he feel?

   B: He has a _____ throat. His throat _____.

5. **A:** What's the matter?

   B: Her toe _____. She has a _____ toe.

6. **A:** What's the matter?

   B: His head _____. He has a _____.

PRACTICE 4

| cook | draw | kick the ball |
| play baseball | play the guitar | sing |

Look at the pictures. Write sentences. Use *can* or *can't* and words in the box.

1. _He can kick the ball._

2. _____

3. _____

4. _____

5. _____

6. _____

PRACTICE 5

Answer the questions. Write *Yes, I can.* or *No, I can't.*

1. Can you play the guitar? _____

2. Can you count to 100 in English? _____

3. Can you cook? _____

4. Can you sing? _____

PRACTICE 6

Look at the pictures. Write questions and answers. Use *can* or *can't.*

1. A: *Can he play basketball?* _____
   B: *Yes, he can.* _____

2. A: _____
   B: _____

3. A: _____
   B: _____

4. A: _____
   B: _____

5. A: _____
   B: _____

Complete the sentences about you and your family.

1. I can _____.

2. I can't _____.

3. My mother can _____.

4. My _____ can't _____.

5. My _____ can _____.

6. My _____ can't _____.

Listen to the conversations and the questions. Circle the correct answers.

Conversation 1

1. a. His name is Daniel.   **b.** His name is Donald.

2. a. His foot hurts.   **b.** His leg hurts.

3. a. He plays baseball.   **b.** He plays basketball.

4. a. Yes, he can.   **b.** No, he can't.

Conversation 2

1. a. Her name is Lili.   **b.** Her name is Laura.

2. a. She feels sad.   **b.** She feels sick.

3. a. She has a backache   **b.** She has a stomachache
and a sore hand.   and a headache.

4. a. Yes, she can.   **b.** No, she can't.

Read about Pedro. Complete his medical form.

My name is Pedro Ruiz. I am sixteen years old. My address is 332 Concord Avenue, Palo Alto, California 94303. My phone number is (415) 555–9912. My mother's name is Sara. My father's name is Victor. My doctor's name is Dr. Stephen Rao. I really feel terrible today. I have a sore throat.

MEDICAL FORM

Name: __Ruiz_____ __Pedro_____ _____
       Last   First   Age

Address: _____
         Street

       _____
         City   State   ZIP Code

Phone: (_____) _____
      Area Code

Father's Name: _____ Mother's Name: _____

Doctor's Name: _____

Reason for seeing the doctor: _____

Read Daniel's medical form. Write about him.

MEDICAL FORM

Name: __Green_____ __Daniel_____ __17_____
       Last   First   Age

Address: __2402 Front Street_____
        Street

       __Erie_____ __Pennsylvania_____ __16511____
         City   State   ZIP Code

Phone: (__814__) __543-0991_____
      Area Code

Father's Name: __Harry_____ Mother's Name: __Alice_____

Doctor's Name: __Dr. Melissa Ito_____

Reason for seeing the doctor: __sore leg_____

His name is _____

_____

_____

_____

Check Your Knowledge

Vocabulary Check

Pretend a part of his body hurts. Write the health problem.

Health Problems

headache	sore foot
stomachache	sore right arm
backache	sore toe
sore throat	sore left arm
sore right leg	sore finger

1. _____sore throat_____
2. _____
3. _____
4. _____
5. _____
6. _____
7. _____
8. _____
9. _____

1.
9.
8.
7.

2.
3.
4.
5.
6.

Check Your Understanding

Complete the questions and answers. Use *can* or *can't*.

1. A: Can Dan play soccer today?

   B: _____No, he can't_____. His leg hurts.

2. A: Can Laura drive?

   B: _____. She's eight years old!

3. A: _____ Ed speak Spanish?

   B: _____. He's from Mexico.

4. A: _____ the students sing?

   B: No, _____.

5. A: _____ go to basketball practice today?

   B: No, I _____. I have a backache and my right arm hurts.

6. A: _____?

   B: Yes, she can. She cooks dinner every day.

PRACTICE 1

apple juice	cheeseburger	french fries
fried chicken	hot dog	milk
pizza	salad	soup

Look at the pictures.
Complete the sentences
with the correct words.

1. I'd like a slice of _____*pizza*_____.

2. Jan wants a _____.

3. Ted wants a bottle of _____.

4. I'd like a _____.

5. Pat wants a _____.

6. Ali wants a bowl of _____.

7. I'd like a carton of _____.

8. Joshua wants three pieces of _____.

9. Bob wants an order of _____.

A. Write the names of the foods.

1. Brian wants a r h u m b a r e g. h (a) m b u r g e r

2. Jeff wants a slice of z a i p z. _ _ _ _ (_)

3. Marcia wants a w h a s d i c n. (_)_ _ _ _ _ _

4. Vicky wants a o t h o g d. _ _ _ (_)_ _

5. Andre wants e p a p l juice. _ _ _(_)_

B. Write the letters in the circles.

— — — — —

C. Complete the answer with the letters in circles.

What does Sylvia want?

She wants a __ __ __ __ __.

Write the prices.

1. three dollars and twenty cents $3.20

2. four dollars and fifty cents   _____

3. seventy-five cents   _____

4. two dollars and sixty-eight cents   _____

5. twenty-five dollars and fifty-nine cents   _____

6. forty-three cents   _____

7. eleven dollars and thirty-five cents   _____

Listen to the conversations. Circle the correct prices.

1.	Hot dog and apple juice	$3.10	($2.97)	$20.90
2.	Chicken and milk	$1.24	$10.42	$2.44
3.	Pizza and apple juice	$4.92	$9.42	$5.89
4.	Small salad	$1.90	$11.90	$1.19
5.	Vegetable soup	$10.75	$1.75	$11.57
6.	Cheeseburgers, fries, and milk	$12.50	$12.05	$20.05

slice	bowl	carton
pieces	bottle	order

A. Complete the price list with words from the box.

PINEWOOD SCHOOL CAFETERIA

1. LARGE ___*bowl*___ OF SOUP $2.15

2. ONE _____ OF PIZZA $1.79

3. LARGE _____ OF FRENCH FRIES $1.15

4. SMALL _____ OF APPLE JUICE $ .85

5. LARGE _____ OF MILK $1.05

6. THREE _____ OF FRIED CHICKEN $2.65

B. Answer the questions. Use *can* or *can't*.

1. Emma has $3.00. Can she buy soup and apple juice? _Yes, she can._____

2. Yoshi has $2.50. Can he buy six pieces of fried chicken? _____

3. Scott has $2.25. Can he buy french fries and milk? _____

4. Louisa has $4.50. Can she buy two pieces of pizza, french fries, and apple juice?

   _____

PRACTICE 6

Complete the orders. Write *a*, *an*, or *some*.

CASHIER: Hi. Can I help you?

TRACY: I'd like **(1.)** _____some_____ vegetable soup and **(2.)** _____ chicken sandwich.

SENG: I'd like **(3.)** _____ small hot dog and **(4.)** _____ apple.

MARTA: I'd like **(5.)** _____ cheeseburger and **(6.)** _____ carton of milk.

NASSIR: I'd like **(7.)** _____ piece of fried chicken and **(8.)** _____ french fries.

OLGA: And I'd like **(9.)** _____ chicken soup, **(10.)** _____ slice of cheese pizza, and **(11.)** _____ apple juice.

RON: I'd like **(12.)** _____ apple, **(13.)** _____ cheese, and **(14.)** _____ milk.

PRACTICE 7

Read the words. Write sentences.

I'd like		order of french fries
Would they like		bowl of soup
Cecilia wants		slice of pizza
I want	a	chicken sandwich
Would you like	an	milk
Frank and Tim want	some	apple
They want		apple juice
Our teacher wants		cheese

1. *I'd like some milk.*

2. _____

3. _____

4. _____

5. _____

6. _____

7. _____

8. _____

PRACTICE 8

Read the questions. Complete the answers.

1. Does Maria have lunch at 12:30?   Yes, _____she does_____.
2. Do you like apple juice?   No, _____.
3. Does Tim like pizza?   Yes, _____.
4. Do they want some soup?   Yes, _____.
5. Does Anna have $10.00?   No, _____.
6. Do you and Kiko like french fries?   No, _____.
7. Do Sue and Jim want hamburgers with their   No, _____.
   french fries?
8. Does Pedro want a cheese sandwich?   No, _____.

PRACTICE 9

A. Read the questions. Write about yourself.

Example:

Do you like pizza? _Yes, I do._____

1. Do you like cheeseburgers? _____
2. Do you like sausage on your pizza? _____
3. Do you have $5.00? _____

B. Read the questions. Ask students in your class. Complete the questions and write the answers.

1. Does _____Maria_____ like milk? _No, she doesn't._____
          (name)

2. Does _____ like hamburgers? _____
          (name)

3. Does _____ like salad? _____
          (name)

4. Does _____ like hot dogs? _____
          (name)

5. Does _____ like pizza? _____
          (name)

6. Does _____ like fried chicken? _____
          (name)

PRACTICE 10

Complete the questions and answers. Write *do, does, doesn't,* or *don't.*

1. A: _____Does_____ Lena want some pizza?

   B: No, she _____.

2. A: _____ you want a hot dog?

   B: Yes, I _____.

3. A: _____ Leroy like french fries?

   B: Yes, he _____.

4. A: _____ Matt and Jason want some milk?

   B: No, they _____.

5. A: _____ your mother have $10.00?

   B: Yes, she _____.

6. A: _____ you and Tony want hot dogs?

   B: Yes, we _____.

PRACTICE 11

Listen to the conversations. Write the names of the foods and the prices.

Food	$
1. hot dog	
2.	
3.	
4.	

Read Nina's and Theo's lunch orders. Look at the menu. Answer the questions.

NINA: I want a chicken sandwich, a large salad, and some milk, please.

THEO: I'd like a hamburger, a small order of french fries, and apple juice, please.

Menu

hamburger.........................$ 2.99

cheeseburger.....................$ 3.49

chicken sandwich..............$ 3.29

cheese sandwich...............$ 2.39

french fries............large $ 1.25
                         small $ .95

salad....................large $2.29
                         small $1.69

carton of milk....................$ .90

apple juice........................$ 1.15

1. What does Nina want for lunch?

_____ $ _____

_____ $ _____

_____ $ _____

Total $ _____

2. What does Theo want for lunch?

_____ $ _____

_____ $ _____

_____ $ _____

Total $ _____

You have $6.75. What would you like for lunch? Look at the menu in Practice 12.
Write the foods and prices. Write the total. Can you buy what you want for lunch?

_____ $ _____

_____ $ _____

_____ $ _____

Total $ _____

Look at Practice 13. What do you want for lunch? How much is it?
Write sentences.

I'd like

Check Your Knowledge

Vocabulary Check

Look at the pictures. Complete the
sentences with the correct words.

apple	apple juice	chicken soup	french fries
fried chicken	hamburger	pizza	salad

1. I'd like a ___hamburger___ and
   some _____.

2. Luisa wants a bowl of _____ and
   an _____.

3. We'd like some cheese _____ and
   some _____.

4. Tony wants two pieces of _____ and
   a small _____.

Check Your Understanding

A. Complete the conversations. Write *a*, *an*, or *some*.

1. **A:** Would you like _____some_____ fried chicken?
   B: No, thank you. I'd like _____ hamburger.
2. **A:** Would you like _____ soup?
   B: Yes, please. I'd like _____ bowl of chicken soup.
3. **A:** Would you like _____ order of french fries?
   B: Yes. I'd like _____ french fries and _____
      hot dog, please.

B. Complete the conversations with *do, does, doesn't,* or *don't*.

1. **A:** _____Does_____ Luisa
      like apples?
   B: Yes, she _____.

2. **A:** _____ you
      and Jane have lunch at 1:30?
   B: No, we _____.

3. **A:** _____ Carlos and
      Lee want some pizza?
   B: Yes, they _____.

4. **A:** _____ Teng like
      cheese?
   B: No, he _____.

PRACTICE 1

Match the pictures with the words. Write the letters.

___d___ **1.** supermarket

_____ **2.** drugstore

_____ **3.** post office

_____ **4.** fire station

_____ **5.** clothing store

_____ **6.** hospital

_____ **7.** bank

_____ **8.** police station

a.

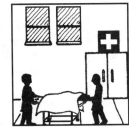
b.

c.

d.

e.

f.

g.

h.

Look at the map. Complete the questions with the names of the buildings.

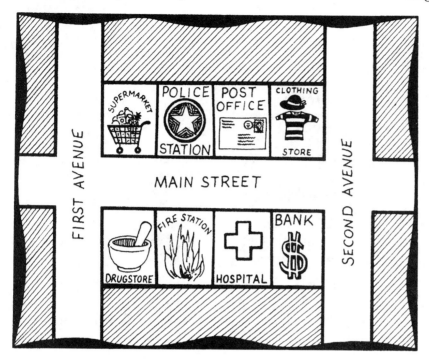

1. **A:** Where's the ___supermarket___?

   B: It's next to the police station. It's on First Avenue.

2. **A:** Where's the _____?

   B: It's between the drugstore and the hospital.

3. **A:** Where's the _____?

   B: It's across from the fire station.

4. **A:** Where's the _____?

   B: It's between the police station and the clothing store.

5. **A:** Where's the _____?

   B: It's on First Avenue. It's next to the fire station.

6. **A:** Where's the _____?

   B: It's past the hospital. It's on the corner of Second Avenue and Main Street.

7. **A:** Where's the _____?

   B: It's across from the post office.

8. **A:** Where's the _____?

   B: It's past the post office. It's on the corner of Main Street and Second Avenue.

PRACTICE 3

Look at the signs. Circle the correct words.

1.   **a.** Telephone   **b.** (Don't go.)   **c.** Go.

2.   **a.** Don't go in.   **b.** Go.   **c.** Restrooms

3.   **a.** Turn left.   **b.** Don't turn left.   **c.** Stop.

4.   **a.** Restrooms   **b.** Don't turn right.   **c.** Telephone

5.   **a.** Don't go in.   **b.** Restrooms   **c.** Turn right.

PRACTICE 4

Read. Circle the correct signs.

1. Don't go.   **a.**   **b.**   **c.**

2. Don't turn right.   **a.**   **b.**   **c.**

3. Boys' restroom   **a.**   **b.**   **c.**

4. Telephone   **a.**   **b.**   **c.**

5. Don't go in.   **a.**   **b.**   **c.**

PRACTICE 5

<table>
<tr><td>across from</td><td>between</td></tr>
<tr><td>next to</td><td>past</td></tr>
</table>

A. Look at the picture. Complete the sentences. Write the correct words.

1. The bank is _____ the park.
2. The library is _____ the park.
3. Van's supermarket is _____ the bank and the drugstore.
4. The shopping mall is _____ the park and the library.
5. The drugstore is _____ the bank and the supermarket.
6. The hospital is _____ the drugstore.
7. The drugstore and the hospital are _____ the shopping mall.

B. Look at the picture in Part A. Read the questions. Write answers. Use *across from*, *between*, *next to*, and *past*.

1. Where's the drugstore? _It's between the supermarket and the hospital._
2. Where's the bank? _____
3. Where's State Street Park? _____
4. Where's the hospital? _____
5. Where's the public library? _____

PRACTICE 6

Complete the conversation with *and* or *or*.

1. A: What do you do on Saturday?

   B: On Saturday, I always do my homework _____*and*_____ go to the park.

2. A: Do you have computer class _____ math class at 1:00?

   B: I have computer class at 1:00.

3. A: Do you have two things in your desk?

   B: Yes, I do. I have a pencil _____ a book.

4. A: Is your mother a librarian _____ a teacher?

   B: She's a teacher.

5. A: How can I get to the school?

   B: Go to the corner of Main Street _____ and First Avenue.

     Turn left _____ walk two blocks.

6. A: Is the school between the fire station _____ the post office?

   B: Yes, it is.

PRACTICE 7

Listen to the conversations. Circle the correct signs.

Draw an X on Fernando's house. Listen to the directions and draw a line on the map. Complete the answer.

Answer: He works at _____.

Look at the map in Practice 8. Answer the questions. Circle *yes* or *no*.

1. Does Fernando walk past First Bank?   yes   (no)
2. Does Fernando walk past the supermarket?   yes   no
3. Does Fernando turn right on Monroe Street?   yes   no
4. Does Fernando walk past the park?   yes   no
5. Does Fernando walk almost five blocks?   yes   no

PRACTICE 10

Look at the map on page 70. Read the directions and answer the question.

On weekdays, Fernando doesn't go home after school. He turns left on Seventh Avenue and walks to the corner of Seventh Avenue and Madison Street. He turns right at the police station and walks one block and turns right on Eighth Avenue. He goes past the fire station and parking garage. He turns left on Washington Street and goes one block. Fernando goes in the building across from the hospital, on the corner of Washington Street and Ninth Avenue.

Where does Fernando go after school? _____

PRACTICE 11

Margaret goes to the library after school, too. How does she get there? Answer the questions. Use the map on page 70.

1. Margaret walks to Ninth Avenue. Does she turn right or left on Washington Street? _____

2. Does she walk one block or two blocks to Ninth Avenue? _____

3. Does she go past the park? _____

4. Does she go past the hospital? _____

5. Does Margaret walk up Eighth Avenue? _____

PRACTICE 12

Look at the map on page 70. Complete the sentences.

To go from the supermarket to Monroe Park, turn right on Seventh
(1.) _____Avenue_____. At the corner of First Bank, turn (2.) _____
on (3.) _____ Street. Go (4.) _____ blocks, and cross
(5.) _____ Avenue. The park is on (6.) _____ Avenue
between (7.) _____ Street and (8.) _____ Street.

PRACTICE 13

Look at the map on page 70. Write directions from the library to the police station.

_____

_____

_____

_____

 **Check Your Knowledge**

Vocabulary Check

Look at the map of Greentree Shopping Mall. Answer the questions. Write the names of the buildings.

Greentree Shopping Mall

LOGAN STREET

DRUG STORE Rx | MUSIC STORE ♫ | BOOK STORE 📖

HOSPITAL ✚ | POLICE STATION

BELL AVENUE

POST OFFICE | LIBRARY | FIRE STATION

CLOTHING STORE | SHOE STORE | BANK $

FOSTER AVENUE

DAKOTA STREET

1. You are in the bookstore on the corner of Bell Avenue and Logan Street. What building is across from you? ___the post office___

2. You are in the building between the post office and the fire station. Where are you? _____

3. You are in a building on Dakota Street. The building is next to the police station. Where are you? _____

4. You are at the police station on the corner of Bell Avenue and Dakota Street. What building is across from you? _____

5. You are on Dakota Street. You turn left on Foster Avenue and walk up the block. Where are you? _____

6. You are on Logan Street. You walk past the post office and the bookstore. You stop at the second building on the left. Where are you? _____

Check Your Understanding

Where is Louisa's friend? Look at the map of Greentree Shopping Mall. Help Louisa follow the directions. Draw a line on the map.

> Walk one block from the drugstore to Bell Avenue. Turn on Bell Avenue and go to Dakota Street. Turn left and walk past the clothing store. Louisa's friend is on the corner of Dakota Street and Foster Avenue.

Louisa's friend is in _____.

WHAT DO THEY DO?

PRACTICE 1

| cashier | doctor | librarian |
| principal | student | teacher |

Look at the pictures. Complete the sentences with the correct words.

1. He's a _____cashier_____.

2. He wants to be a _____.

3. He's a _____.

4. She wants to be a _____.

5. She's a _____.

6. He's wants to be a _____.

Occupations		**Verbs**	
bus driver	nurse	delivers	picks up
dentist	police officer	drives	protects
firefighter	salesperson	fixes	puts out
mail carrier		helps	sells

What do they do? Complete the sentences with the correct occupations and verbs.

1. She's a ___police officer___. She ___protects___ people.

2. She's a _____. She _____ sick people.

3. He's a _____. He _____ teeth.

4. He's a _____. He _____ a bus.

5. She's a _____. She _____ and _____ mail.

6. He's a _____. He _____ fires.

7. He's a _____. He _____ TVs.

PRACTICE 3

Where do they work?

Match each person to the place. Write the names of the buildings.

_____ **1.** firefighter

_____ **2.** mail carrier

_____ **3.** salesperson

_____ **4.** teacher

_____ **5.** police officer

_____ **6.** doctor

a.  _____

b.  _____

c.  _____fire station_____

d.  _____

e.  _____

f.  _____

PRACTICE 4

Write the plural forms of the nouns.

1. librarian _____librarians_____   **5.** doctor _____

2. nurse _____   **6.** police officer _____

3. bus driver _____   **7.** dentist _____

4. firefighter _____   **8.** salesperson _____

PRACTICE 5

Complete the sentences with *like* or *likes* and the infinitive of a word in the box.

draw	go	listen	play
read	talk	write	

1. Carl ___likes to draw___ pictures.

2. Marvin _____ to school.

3. Maya and Sofia _____ basketball.

4. Anna _____ to music.

5. Bill and Gerry _____ books.

6. Diana _____ to her teacher.

7. Rob _____ letters to his friends.

PRACTICE 6

Read the answers. Write questions with *What*.

1. **A:** *What does she like to do* _____ ?

   B: She likes to play baseball.

2. **A:** _____ ?

   B: I want to be a bus driver.

3. **A:** _____ ?

   B: He wants to read a book.

4. **A:** _____ ?

   B: I like to listen to music.

PRACTICE 7

Use the words to write sentences. You don't have to use a word from each column.

I You Maria Reiko and Paul Our teacher Doctors My mother The students	(don't) (doesn't)	like likes want wants	to go to draw to listen to write to eat to play to help to do	students people basketball homework swimming to school pizza to music

1. *Maria doesn't like to write.* _____

2. _____

3. _____

4. _____

5. _____

6. _____

7. _____

8. _____

Read the questions. Write answers with *because*.

1. Why does Rose want to be a librarian?
  Because she likes books.

2. Why does Mina want to be a firefighter?

_____

3. Why does David want to go to the park?

_____

4. Why does Luis want to go to the gym?

_____

 Listen to the sentences. Circle **T** for true or **F** for false.

1.	T	(F)	**5.**	T	F
2.	T	F	**6.**	T	F
3.	T	F	**7.**	T	F
4.	T	F	**8.**	T	F

Read about André Mamet and complete the chart.

This is André Mamet. His father is a police officer. He likes his job because he likes to protect people. His mother is a nurse. She works at Children's Hospital. She likes her job because she likes to help sick children. André doesn't want to be a nurse. He doesn't like hospitals. He wants to be a math teacher because he likes math. He wants to help students, too.

Name	Occupation	Reason for Occupation (Why?)
Mr. Mamet	*police officer*	
Mrs. Mamet		
André		

PRACTICE 11

A. Join André's sentences with *and*, *but*, or *because*.

1. My father is a police officer. My mother is a nurse.

   My father is a police officer, and my mother is a nurse.

2. My father helps people. My mother helps people, too.

   _____

3. My parents like their jobs. They like to help people.

   _____

4. I want to help people. I don't want to be a nurse.

   _____

5. I don't want to be a nurse. I don't like hospitals.

   _____

6. I like math. I want to help students, too.

   _____

B. Write sentences about your family. Use *and*, *but*, and *because*.

   _____

   _____

   _____

   _____

Check Your Knowledge

Vocabulary Check

Complete the sentences. Use words from the box.

bus driver	delivers
dentist	drives
firefighter	fixes
mail carrier	puts out
salesperson	sells
principal	protects
police officer	helps

1. A _____bus driver_____ _____drives_____ a bus.

2. A _____ _____ mail to people.

3. A _____ _____ teeth.

4. A _____ _____ things in a store.

5. A _____ _____ fires.

6. A _____ _____ students and teachers.

7. A _____ _____ people.

Check Your Understanding

A. Read about Ramón and Lucy. Answer the questions. Write complete sentences.

Ramón wants to be a firefighter. He wants to help people, and he likes to put out fires. His friend Lucy wants to be a PE teacher because she likes to play soccer and baseball. On the weekends, she always plays basketball in the park. She likes to work with students and help them, too.

1. What does Lucy want to be?

   _____

2. Why does she like this occupation?

   _____

3. What does Ramón want to be?

   _____

4. Why does he like this occupation?

   _____

B. What do you want to be? Why? Write your answer in complete sentences.

_____

_____

_____

_____

PRACTICE 1

Look at the pictures. Circle the word or words.

1. (jogging)   swimming   studying

2. playing a   playing Frisbee   playing soccer
   computer game

3. swimming   skating   jogging

4. playing Frisbee   working out   playing a computer game

5. studying   writing letters   skating

6. skating   playing soccer   playing Frisbee

7. doing homework   playing a   working out
   computer game

8. swimming   jogging   riding a bike

catching	hitting	kicking	running
throwing	playing football	playing softball	

What are they doing?

Complete the sentences. Use words from the box.

1. He's _____kicking_____ the ball.

2. He's _____ with the ball.

3. They're _____.

4. She's _____ the ball.

5. She's _____ the ball.

6. They're _____.

7. She's _____ the Frisbee.

PRACTICE 3

Complete the sentences. Write the *-ing* form of the verbs.

1. Ron and Eva are _____*studying*_____ in the library. (**study**)
2. Luis is _____ a book at school. (**read**)
3. Hannah and Mariko are _____ their homework at home. (**do**)
4. Jamal and Ed are _____ football in the park. (**play**)
5. Reiko is _____ at the gym. (**work out**)
6. Nora and Tammy are _____ pizza at the Pizza Place. (**eat**)

PRACTICE 4

Complete the puzzle with the *-ing* form of the verbs.

Across

1. kick
3. skate
5. throw
7. get
8. use
10. play
12. jog

Down

2. catch
3. swim
4. run
6. write
9. say
11. go

Look at the pictures. Answer the questions. Ask questions with *What.*

Takeo

1. **A:** What's Takeo doing?
   B: *He's studying.* **or** *He's reading.*

2. **A:** What's Carmen doing?
   B: _____

   Carmen

3. **A:** What are Danny and Kevin doing?
   B: _____

Danny and Kevin

4. **A:** What's Karla doing?
   B: _____

   Karla

5. **A:** What are Mark and Karim doing?
   B: _____

Mark and Karim

6. **A:** _____
   B: They're working out.

   Brian and Tomás

7. **A:** _____
   B: _____

Susan

8. **A:** _____
   B: _____

   Travis and Dina

PRACTICE 6

Read the questions. Complete the answers.

1. **A:** Is Juan riding his bike now?
   B: No, _____*he isn't*_____.

2. **A:** Are Julie and Allen playing basketball?
   B: Yes, _____.

3. **A:** Is Sandra playing basketball, too?
   B: Yes, _____.

4. **A:** Are Bao and Calvin jogging?
   B: No, _____.

5. **A:** Are you reading now?
   B: Yes, _____.

6. **A:** Are you and Freddie studying English?
   B: Yes, _____.

7. **A:** Are you writing a letter?
   B: No, _____.

8. **A:** Are you and Megan eating now?
   B: No, _____.

PRACTICE 7

Look at the pictures. Complete the conversations.

1. **A:** _____*Is*_____ Takeo _____*studying*_____ now? **(study)**
   B: No, he _____. He _____ his bike. **(ride)**

2. **A:** _____ Bill and Noriko _____ in the library? **(study)**
   B: Yes, they _____. They _____ their homework. **(do)** He _____ a book. **(read)** She _____. **(write)**

3. **A:** _____ Jen and Gary _____? **(skate)**
   B: No, they _____. They _____ a game in the park. **(play)** She _____ a ball. **(hit)** He _____ it. **(catch)**

4. **A:** _____ Ms. Brito _____? **(swim)**
   B: Yes, she _____. Ms. Brito and the students _____ in the pool. **(swim)** They _____ fun. **(have)**

PRACTICE 8

| doing homework | playing football | skating |
| working | working out | |

Listen to the conversation. What is each person doing? Write the activity in the chart.

Name	Activity
1. Chung	*playing football*
2. Pedro	
3. Dave	
4. Cindy's mother	
5. Cindy's father	
6. Anna	
7. Cindy	

PRACTICE 9

Read the letter. Complete the chart on page 87.

June 7, _____

Dear Brittany,

Hi! It's a beautiful day. I'm at the park with my friends Jon and Lisa. They're playing baseball, but I'm writing letters. I'm not playing because I have a sore leg. My sisters are at the park, too. Lydia is jogging, and Isabel and Kate are playing Frisbee. My brother Simon and my parents aren't at the park. Simon is playing a computer game at home, and my mother and father are having lunch at a restaurant.

How are you? What are you doing? What are the people in your family doing?

Write soon.

Your friend,
Linda

Name	Activity
1. Linda	writing letters
2. Jon	
3.	playing baseball
4.	jogging
5. Isabel	
6.	playing Frisbee
7. Simon	
8. Linda's parents	

PRACTICE 10

You are in a park with your friends. What are you doing? What are your friends doing? Write a letter to a friend or a family member. Use a greeting, a closing, and today's date.

Check Your Knowledge

Vocabulary Check

What are the people doing?

Write a sentence for each picture. Use *He's*, *She's*, or *They're* and the present progressive form of the verbs in the box.

hit a ball	jog	kick a ball
play softball	ride bikes	skate
swim	throw a Frisbee	

1. He's kicking a ball.

2. _____

3. _____

4. _____

Check Your Understanding

A. Read the letter. Write answers to the questions.

> Dear Pat,
>
> Hi! How are you? What are you doing today? It's Saturday morning, and I'm at the library with my friend Carmen. She's studying, but I'm not studying now. I'm writing letters. My brothers, Eric and Steve, are at the pool. They're swimming. My sister Gina is with them, but she isn't swimming. She's reading at the pool. My friend James is playing baseball at the park, and my father is at the gym. He's working out.
>
> How's your family? Where are your friends? What is everyone doing now?
>
> Write soon.
>
> Your friend,
> Alicia

1. Is Carmen writing letters? No, she isn't. She's studying.

2. Are Eric and Steve swimming? _____

3. Is Gina swimming? _____

4. Is James working out? _____

5. What's Alicia's father doing? _____

6. What's Alicia doing? _____

B. You are Pat. Write a letter in your notebook to Alicia. Answer her questions. Write about your family and friends and what you are doing now.

PRACTICE **1**

jacket	jeans	shirt	shoes
skirt	socks	sweater	T-shirt
pants	blouse	sneakers	dress

Look at the picture. Write the correct word from the box.

1. _____jacket_____
2. _____
3. _____
4. _____
5. _____
6. _____
7. _____
8. _____

big	small
long	short

Look at the pictures. Complete the sentences. Use the correct word from the box.

1. I can't wear this T-shirt! It's too _____small_____ for me.

2. Betsy likes those shoes, but they're too _____ for her.

3. That dress is too _____ for Keiko. She can't wear it.

4. You can't buy those jeans. They're too _____!

5. This sweater is too _____! I don't want to buy it.

6. You can't wear that jacket! It's too _____ for you.

7. I like these pants, but they're too _____ for me.

PRACTICE 3

People are giving their opinions about clothes. Complete the sentences with the correct words.

1. I'd like to buy this blue jacket. I think it's _____*beautiful*_____.
(**beautiful/ugly**)

2. I don't want that orange and purple sweater. It's _____.
(**great/ugly**)

3. These sneakers are _____, but they're too small.
(**great/awful**)

4. I want to buy this green dress. I think it's _____.
(**ugly/pretty**)

5. I think that yellow skirt is _____. Don't buy it.
(**nice/awful**)

6. This hat is _____, but its too big!
(**ugly/nice**)

PRACTICE 4

Compete the sentences with a word from the box.

this	these
that	those

1. ____*This*____ shirt is great.

2. _____ shirt is awful.

3. I don't want _____ shoes.

4. I want _____ shoes.

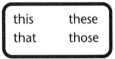

5. _____ jeans are awful.

6. _____ jeans are great.

7. I'd like to buy _____ hat.

8. _____ hat is ugly!

PRACTICE 5

Complete the sentences. Write the correct words.

1. I'd like to buy _____*this*_____ tan shirt. How much is it?
   (this/these)

2. I think _____ pants are nice. Do you like the color?
   (this/these)

3. _____ white sneakers are great, but they're too big!
   (That/Those)

4. Don't buy _____ red hat. I think it's awful.
   (that/those)

5. I like _____ T-shirt, but it's too small for me.
   (this/these)

6. Do you like _____ blue jeans?
   (this/these)

7. How much is _____ dress?
   (that/those)

8. I'd like _____ blouse, but I don't like _____ shoes.
   (this/these)   **(that/those)**

PRACTICE 6

Listen to Rosa. What are the people wearing? Complete the sentences.

   a   an   black   blue   shoes   sneakers

1. Taka is wearing _____*a*_____ blue T-shirt, _____ jeans,
   and black _____.

   a   an   big   black   shirt   skirt

2. Pat is wearing _____ tan jacket and a brown _____.
   Pat has a _____ book bag, too.

   gray   green   jeans   pants   shirt   skirt

3. Lee is wearing a _____ sweater, a gray-and-white
   _____, and black _____.

   a   an   long   shirt   small   tan   T-shirt

4. Rosa is wearing a white _____, _____ orange
   sweater, and a _____ skirt. She has a _____ book bag.

Melinda Harris is ordering some clothes from the Springo catalogue. She
is circling the things she wants to buy. Melinda lives at 266 Prospect Avenue,
San Francisco, California 94132. Her phone number is (415) 670-3756.

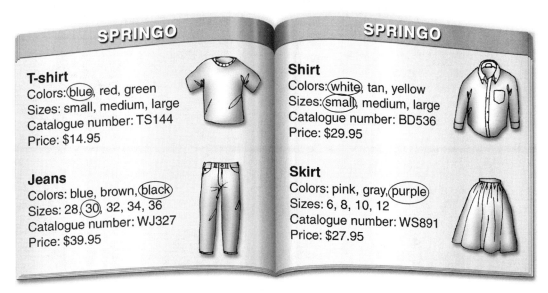

SPRINGO

T-shirt
Colors: (blue), red, green
Sizes: small, medium, large
Catalogue number: TS144
Price: $14.95

Jeans
Colors: blue, brown, (black)
Sizes: 28, (30), 32, 34, 36
Catalogue number: WJ327
Price: $39.95

SPRINGO

Shirt
Colors: (white), tan, yellow
Sizes: (small), medium, large
Catalogue number: BD536
Price: $29.95

Skirt
Colors: pink, gray, (purple)
Sizes: 6, 8, 10, 12
Catalogue number: WS891
Price: $27.95

Complete the catalogue order form for Melinda.

Springo Clothing Company

Name: _____
         LAST   FIRST

Address: _____
          STREET   CITY   STATE   ZIP

Phone Number: _____
               AREA CODE

HOW MANY	CATALOGUE NUMBER	CLOTHING ITEM	SIZE	COLOR	PRICE
1	TS144	T-shirt	small	blue	$14.95

TOTAL _____

Look at the catalogue in Practice 7. Choose one thing to order. Answer the
questions. Write sentences.

   1. What do you want to order? _I'd like_ _____

   2. What is the catalogue number? _____

   3. What size and color do you want? _____

   4. What is the price? _____

Vocabulary Check

Look at the pictures. Complete the sentences with the correct words.

jacket	pants	shirt	socks
big	small	skirt	shoes
sweater	T-shirt	long	short

1. I'd like to buy these _____*shoes*_____ and _____.

2. I want to buy a black _____ and a white _____.

3. This _____ is too _____!

4. This _____ is too _____!

5. I don't want these _____. They're too _____!

Check Your Understanding

A. Correct these sentences.

    1. This black jeans is great.

    2. Do you like that purpel sweter?

    3. I'd like to buy this brown shoes.

    4. These blue dress is beutiful.

    5. I like this oranje T-shirt, but it's to small for me.

B. What are you wearing today? Write sentences.

_____

_____